Dry Rivers and Standing Rocks

University of New Mexico Press

Albuquerque

Dry Rivers and Standing Rocks

A Word Finder for the American West

by Scott Thybony

Library of Congress

Cataloging-in-Publication Data

Thybony, Scott.

Dry Rivers and Standing Rocks : a word finder for
the American West / Scott Thybony. — 1st ed.

    p. cm.

  ISBN 0-8263-2260-3 (alk. paper)

  ISBN 0-8263-2261-1 (pbk. : alk. paper)

   1. English language — Dialects — West (U.S.) —
Glossaries, vocabularies, etc. 2. Western stories —
Authorship. 3. Americanisms — West (U.S.) 4. West
(U.S.) — Terminology. I. Title.

PE2970.W4 T48 2000

427'.978 — dc21   00-008471

Illustrations: Clarence E. Dutton, *Tertiary History of the
Grand Cañon District*, Government Printing Office, 1882

Design: Malcolm Grear Designers

Contents

Introduction

Writer's block can begin with a single word, a prospect faced by Gustave Flaubert many times. The French novelist spent months searching for the right word. "When he was at his desk, looking at a page of first draft," wrote his friend Emile Zola, "he would hold his head in his hands and stare at the page for minutes on end as if he had mesmerized it. He would drop his pen, he would not speak, but remain absorbed, lost in the search for an elusive word or a construction whose mechanism escaped him."

It can happen to the most careful writers—especially the careful ones. You find yourself stuck, staring at a sentence dangling in mid-air, unable to think of a single word to anchor it. You thumb through a thesaurus, or double-click and point and click again, only to turn up a string of vaguely similar words. But nothing works, especially if you're writing about the West, a different flavor from the standard New York-London fare. You leave a blank and go on, hoping it will sneak up on you later. Often it doesn't.

To cure a case of the blank stares, I started a file on the principle of when in doubt, throw all your notes in a folder and stick a label on it. When I interviewed someone—rancher, river guide, recovering writer—I paid attention to the color and texture of the language, listening for grounded talk. I learned to give the same attention to my reading, watching for place-linked words, both rooted and wind-blown. Whatever flowed, whatever threw sparks made it into the file. The practice was a way of learning to see the vast, broken spaces west of the 98th meridian, a coming to terms with the dry side of the continent.

After a while, I got tired of picking through the scraps and trying to decipher old scrawls each time I needed a word. So between assignments I consolidated the odds and ends onto a computer file. After a workable sorting, I ended up with a list of western toponymns, cowboyisms, American Indian words on permanent loan, Spanish terms, usually anglicized, a sprinkling of Arabic tossed in for seasoning, various scientific terms for added ballast, random coinings, borrowings, and outright expropriations, and even slang when it worked better than Webster's English. The file grew into something resembling a thesaurus of western geography.

Look up the word "thesaurus" in a thesaurus, and you'll find a run of words along these lines: lexicon, phrase book, synonym finder, vocabulary, word bank, word book, word cache, word depository, word list, word vault—the list keeps growing until it gets out of hand. Follow a word far enough and the language begins to unravel. So I've set a few limits. What you won't find here is a comprehensive collection or scholarly approach. Language needs room to breathe, and it has plenty of it here. The compilation contains paired words like "standing rock," grafts like "snaggletooth," and loners like "hoodoo." I've left out words so common they no longer click. Dead links. And I've added words out of circulation long enough to get recharged. Try "yonder," a word compressing the history of the West into a single longing.

The most useful words aren't those you think you need. At some point I realized the blank page in front of me wasn't due to a lack of vocabulary but a loss of motion. My thinking had high-centered, and I needed something to nudge me out of the rut. Words with traction. The right word, one with a certain timbre, could carry my thinking in the direction it needed to go. Another use for this compilation is to avoid repetition, to find a word just a shade different from the one I've already worked to death. So you'll find two kinds of words here: nudgers and shaders. These are divided into several categories: forms, traits, and motion—roughly equivalent to nouns, modifiers, and verbs but without being confined to set definitions. These groupings narrow the search effort, while many entries also include a few quotes to widen the horizons. Some days you need both.

These short quotes generally reflect what I was reading on a particular assignment rather than a best-of-the West list. This leaves out many good writers. Sometimes only a single phrase caught my attention in an otherwise flat read, so a quote isn't an endorsement of an entire work. Also, the nature of writing tends to encourage cannibalism. Writers consume the words of their own kind and sometimes swallow without chewing. I haven't tried to find the first use of a phrase, only where I first ran across it. I'll leave it to others to trace the food chain. Because this selection evolved without conscious intent, it has a certain Darwinian randomness to it with lots of chance mutations. I didn't read books with the idea of finding words to add to the list. They emerged from my research and interviews, giving them a practical focus from the start. The result is a literary crowbar, a tool to pry out stubborn ideas.

Landscape generates its own vernacular. Linguistically raw, the West continues to serve as a catalyst for a new American vocabulary. But much of what we think of as regional has tumbled in from somewhere else, like many of the current residents. From the start, European arrivals groped for ways to express a landscape far beyond their collective experience. And they still do. A German hitchhiker I picked up looked out the window at an aspen grove. Struggling for words to describe the chalky-white bark, he finally said, "Very tasty."

Where does a newcomer find words to match the vast distances, the nameless shapes of eroded rock, the scent of rain slapping dust? Those whose perceptions have been formed by other vistas "enter this strange region with a shock," wrote Clarence

Dutton more than a century ago. The Yale-trained geologist acknowledged the limits of his scientific vocabulary, and once in the field began applying an overlay of architectural terms. Buttes became temples and towers; cliffs became façades and curtain walls. Realizing a need to go beyond the geologic, Captain Dutton set aside his scientific detachment and dictated dramatic, chapter-long descriptions. "The Panorama from Point Sublime" runs for seventeen pages and became a Grand Canyon classic. In this region, he wrote, "the geologist finds himself a poet."

Even a straight-forward term like "canyon" doesn't fit all the landforms it's called on to cover. English speakers adopted it, among many others, from the Spanish spoken by New Mexicans who had lived in place for generations. It works for a setting like Canyon de Chelly where a stream meanders across a flat floor tucked between perpendicular cliffs. But a geologic event like the Grand Canyon is too vast and complex to fit the same category and bears little resemblance to Bryce Canyon, an amphitheater gnawed from the rim of a plateau. Other borrowings work better because they fit specific landforms. Geologists use the Spanish word, *cuesta*, for a ridge with a gentle slope on one side and a steep scarp on the other. Even the sound of it hints at its meaning. Reading the word "cuesta," I see a rising swell of ground breaking like a wave in a crest of bare rock. Another geologic term, hogback, also refers to a cliff-topped ridge, but this one slopes steeply on both sides. It lacks the Spanish grace but bristles with a certain frontier force.

Many American Indian words connect directly with the land in a way I like. Some translations I've let stand alone without the indigenous word. For example, under the heading "dry rain" you'll find the Hopi expression "standing rain" but not, *yoy-wunuto*, or the literal translation "rain goes to stand." That reflects my own limitations, I guess. Native American words sit heavily on the tongues of certain English speakers. When living with a Navajo family, I made the attempt to speak properly and give each word the right inflection. But they couldn't hold back their laughs for long—especially the women. When I asked what it was I had said, they usually told me, "Something dirty."

Language is too fluid to nail down and changes rapidly when isolated. Cut off for a couple of weeks on a long river trip, you begin speaking in tongues. Your vocabulary becomes ingrown. Tears roll down your face at the same joke that leaves someone from another river party staring at you in disbelief. When you reach the take-out, the shuttle driver sits behind the wheel, cut off from the conversation, unable to make any sense of what you're saying. A few of these words have slipped onto the list. It's usually disposable language, forgotten by the next trip—unless you're taking notes.

Like a hand-drawn map, this compilation has the common distortion of emphasizing the home turf. Word density tends to cluster around the

Colorado Plateau and the wider Southwest before extending up the Rockies. The coverage begins to thin as it spills into the Great Basin on one side and the Great Plains on the other, and it gets real light by the time it reaches the coastal ranges. These words accumulated during assignments from Mexico to the interior of British Columbia, but in between I missed the Pacific West. Whatever corner of the region these words come from, they share a common ground. Open the list at random and begin reading. The words sound like an incantation. Even loosely strung together, they have a certain cadence, their own rough poetry.

The original file began with a selection of words I found interesting and ended as a tool with the right heft and balance for the work I do. It's not perfect, but remember Flaubert. He demanded a perfect fit from something inherently loose-jointed. His writing stiffened, and he began to dread words. "Slowly," Zola wrote, "from the legs to the waist, then to the head, Flaubert turned to marble." Out here it would have been Navajo sandstone.

LAND

landscape

___

forms

backdrop, brushland, canyonscape, cliffland,
countryside, desert highland, dryland, landmass,
panhandle, rimland, rockscape, scrabland, scrub-
land, setting, surroundings, terrain, topography,
western reaches

___

baldrock country, black sand country, brush country,
canyon country, cactus country, elemental country,
elevated country, high country, hill country,
mesa country, mountain country, plateau country,
redrock country, rim country, sandhill country,
slickrock country, upcountry, upside-down country,
west country

___

traits

aeolian (eolian), arid, bedrock, chaotic, chromatic,
convoluted, deep, deeper, denuded, geometric,
harsh, intermontane, lithic, luminous, lunar, mythic,
natural, rawboned, revelatory, rock-floored, rough-
hewn, sapless, semiarid, shamanic, solitary, spare,
stark, sun-drenched, sunstruck, surreal, tabular,
visionary, waterless, windswept

___

la frontera "the borderlands"

Edward Abbey, writer: *"moon-dead landscape,"* **Edward Dahlberg**, poet: *"vast, unconscious geography,"* **Frederick Dellenbaugh**, surveyor: *"kaleidoscopic topography,"* **Jay Dusard**, photographer: *"articulated by light,"* **D. H. Lawrence**, novelist: *"And in old landscapes, as in old people, the flesh wears away, and the bones become prominent,"* **N. Scott Momaday**, writer: *"the remembered earth,"* **Taylor Thompson**, Texas ranger: *"a large scope of territory"*

region

corner, district, domain, locale, locus, province, quadrant, quarter, range, reach, territory, tract, zone

legends

Harahey, Lake Bonneville, Northwest Passage, Quivira, River of the West, San Buenaventura River, Seven Cities of Cibola, Sierra Azul

wilderness

forms
backcountry, backlands, back reaches, blank spot on the map, boondocks, boonies, hardscrabble, hardscramble, Hell's hippocket, hideaway, high lonesome, hinterlands, old ground, outback, refuge, rock wilderness, roughlands, sanctuary, solitudes, tall uncut, the tules, vacant land, wasteland, wildlands

traits
cliff-girt, empty, impenetrable, remote, roadless,
trackless, uncharted, unparcelled, untenanted,
untrammeled

Hopi: "gray earth" (barrenlands)

---

despoblado "uninhabited lands," *el cuartelejo*
"the far quarter"
ultima deserta

Edward Abbey, writer: *"the edge of nowhere,"* **Loren
Eiseley**, anthropologist: *"vast drifts of stone and gravel,"*
Lao-tzu, philosopher: *"the nameless wild,"* **Cormac
McCarthy**, novelist: *"a region electric and wild,"*
Archibald MacLeish, poet: *"the elsewhere that is holy,"*
Friedrich Nietzsche, philosopher: *"tasting strange
air in strange lands,"* **John Wesley Powell**, explorer:
"the Great Unknown" and *"a vast wilderness of rocks,"*
Henry David Thoreau, writer: *"unappropriated land"*

expanse

---

forms
absolute distance, blank immensity, cavernous
space, fastness, immense span, null distance, raw
space, reach, sweep, the blue distance, vacant
distance, vast field, vastness

---

traits
boundless, dead-flat, endless, far-and-wide,
immeasurable, infinite, large-caliber, limitless,
measureless, mind-numbing, rock-cut, sun-baked,
sunlit, unbounded, unfettered, unlimited, vast,
wild, wind-buffeted

Edward Abbey, writer: *"a great vast aching vacancy of pure space,"* and *"a vast well of space,"* **Ambrose Bierce**, journalist: *"the measureless reaches of the West,"* **Clarence Dutton**, geologist: *"a troubled sense of immensity,"* **Susanne Langer**, philosopher: *"Our sense of space is gravitational as much as visual,"* **D. H. Lawrence**, novelist: *"the great, hollow, rock-wilderness space,"* **T. E. Lawrence**, soldier: *"a great emptiness,"* **Pierre Loti**, traveler: *"naked emptiness"* and *"the bleak enormity,"* **Friedrich Nietzsche**, philosopher: *"deep light-distances,"* **Walter Clement Powell**, surveyor: *"the immense surface of earth and sky,"* **J. B. Priestley**, writer: *"vast crystalline spaces"*

vista

forms
aspect, field of vision, lookoff, lookout, observation point, overlook, panorama, pulloff, pullout, turnout, vantage point, viewpoint

traits
broad, cliff-framed, cliff-rimmed, commanding, deep, full-circle, heat-bleached, panoramic, sweeping, uninterrupted, unobstructed

horizon

celestial horizon, cliffline, crestline, curve of the world, earthline, earth's curvature, the extreme distance, false horizon, local horizon (visible horizon), pure line, ridgeline, skyline, true horizon

traits
backlit, blank, bright, fixed, long

Cheyenne: "the blue vision," Plains Indian: *waho* "great circle of the horizon"

Stephen Crane, writer: *"the horizon, a precipice,"* **Gustave Flaubert**, novelist: *"unreachable horizon,"* **Tom Lea**, writer: *"lost edge of the world,"* **Cormac McCarthy**, novelist: *"unseen rim"* and *"the trembling perimeter of the world,"* **Frank Waters**, writer: *"haunting sweep of illimitable horizons"*

canyon

forms
blind canyon, box canyon, inner canyon, hanging canyon, hidden canyon, outer canyon, saw-cut canyon, stair-step canyon

abyss, channel, chasm, chute, cleft, declivity, defile, depths, drainageway, excavation, geologic maze, gorge, gulch, gulf, gullet, inverted mountain, labyrinth, maze, mazeway, rock depths, transept, void

downcanyon, upcanyon

traits
cloud-covered, constricted, crooked, hydra-headed, inaccessible, interlaced, interlocking, intricate, labyrinthine, many-armed, perpendicular, profound, riven, serpentine, sinuate, sinuous, sculptural, sheer-walled, storm-carved, straight up-and-down, tangled, tortuous, twisting, unnamed, vascular, vertical-walled

motion
bend, bifurcate, bisect, contort, curl, descend, drop, fall, knife, meander, plunge, reach down, sink, slash, snake, split, stairstep, step downward, twine, twist, wind

Navajo: *biko, bokho* "canyon," *tsegi, tseyi'* "among the rocks, within the rock, or high rock"

barranca, cahon (cajon) "box canyon," *cañada* "canyon or small glen," *cañoncito* "little canyon"

Dante, poet: *"depthless Deep" and "desolate chasm,"* **Clarence Dutton**, geologist: *"illimitable depths" and "bewildering mazes,"* **Colin Fletcher**, writer: *"cleaving space,"* **Herbert Gregory**, geologist: *"tortuously winding courses,"* **John Milton**, poet: *"the dark, unbottomed, infinite Abyss,"* **John Wesley Powell**, explorer: *"our granite prison" (Inner Gorge, Grand Canyon)*

bend

close-set curves, compound curves (recurving loops), compressed loops, crook, elbow, enclosed meander, entrenched meander, gooseneck, horse-shoe, incised meander, meanderings, ingrown meander, kink, loop, oxbow, rincon (abandoned meander, corner), turnings

junction

forms
confluence, convergence, intersection, juncture, nexus

motion
converge, intersect, join, merge, meet

Gary Snyder, poet: *"A 'doab' is the spit of land where two rivers come together."*

side canyon

arm, branch, fork, glen (narrow side canyon), offshoot, prong, stem, side-draw, transept

cross canyon (bisects main canyon), feeder canyon, lateral canyon, secondary canyon, second-order canyon, subcanyon, tributary canyon

Herbert Gregory, geologist: *"box-headed tributary"*

slot canyon

forms
catacomb, cleavage, cleft, constriction, corkscrew, corridor, crack, dive, elliptical chamber, finger canyon, gash, hallway, hidden chamber, hollow, incision, narrows, passageway, ventricle

traits
cavernous, convoluted, ethereal, flaring, fluted, keyhole, scalloped, sinuous, snarly

Navajo: "slim canyon"

John Wesley Powell, explorer: *"one wall overhangs the other"*

cliff

forms
band, bluff, buffalo jump, bulwark, cliff profile, cliffrock, cliffside, clifftop, escarpment, façade, fault scarp, heights, mural front, meander spur, overcliff, palisade, parapet, precipice, rampart, reef, rib, ribbing, rock face, scarp, skyscraper rock, tier

barrier wall, blank wall, cathedral wall, curtain wall, facewall, headwall, mural wall, sidewall, tapestry wall

blade, fin, free-standing wall, leaf, upright slab, wing

---

traits
bold, bouldered, concave, convex, cross-hatched, encircling, enclosing, encompassing, even-crested, faceted, flat-faced, fluted, hatchet-edged, laminated, layer-cake, massing, massive, ogee-curved (S-shaped), overhanging, painted, pocked, perpendicular, receding, retreating, ribbed, rounding, scarped, sheared, sheer, sinuous, terraced, thundering, tiered, undercut, undermined, upthrusting, unscalable, wind-fluted, wind-pocked, wind-whittled

---

motion
ascend, climb, descend, drop, dropoff, fall, hang, jut, lift, loom, pitch up, rear, rise, stack, surge, terminate, thrust, upcast, uplift, upthrust, vault

---

Edward Abbey, writer: *"dragon-tooth reef,"* **Clarence Dutton**, geologist: *"the vast maze of cliffwork,"* **Everett Ruess**, artist: *"sheer incurving cliffs"*

rim

forms
brim, brink, brow, caprock, capstone, clifftop, crest, crestline, dropoff, lip, margin, raw edge, rimrock, slick rim (rounded cliff), slip-off slope, threshold, tipoff, verge

traits
abrupt, burred, crenate, crenellated, eroded, flared, knurled, outer, utter

Havasupai: *wikatata,* "rough rim," Navajo: *tsédáá'* "rim"

William Shakespeare, playwright: *"the extreme verge"*

promontory

cape, headland, meander core, molar, nose, outlier, point, projection, prominence, protrusion, prow, salient, snout, spur, tip

dry fall

barrier fall, boulder jam, chokestone, dropoff, jump, jump-up, nick point, pouroff, step down

ledge

forms
catwalk, covered shelf, horizontal molding, landing, ledgerock, microledge, perch, platform, purchase, rocky flange, shelf, sill

traits
broken, crumbly, over-hanging, projecting, tapering,
unbroken, undercut

motion
pinchout, taper

Hopi: *tuuwi* "cliff ledge"

break

chimney, cleft, crack, cranny, crevice, furrow,
groove, gullet, joint, rift, rupture, seam, shaft, slit,
splitrock (kernsprung), transverse crack, trench

alcove

forms
amphitheater, bay, bowl, cathedral vault, cavity,
chamber, concavity, cove, echo hall, eye socket,
embayment, glen, grotto, honeycomb rock, maw,
niche, nook, pocket, recessed wall, swallow hole
(weathering along strata), vault

overhang, pictograph shelter, rock shelter (near-cave),
ruin-sheltering cave, shelter cave, sheltering cliff,
sheltering rock

foothold, handhold, toehold

traits
arched, band-shell, cavernous, eggshell, gaping,
scalloped

Herbert Gregory, geologist: *"cliff pocket, fish mouth,
owl hole, and sky hole"*

arch

aperture, blind arch, blind window, bridge, free-standing arch, hole-in-the-rock, natural bridge, perforation, royal arch, skylight, span, window

standing rock

hoodoo

effigy, gargoyle, goblin, hobgoblin, snaggletooth

Bob Dye, river guide: *"who-done-it"*

monolith

forms
balanced rock, bobbin, cenotaph, column, ear, earth pillar, fang, finger, gnomon (sundial indicator), horn, longstone, minaret, monument, needle, obelisk, pillar, sentinel, spire, stack, statuary, thumb, tooth, totem pole, tower, turret, tusk, volcanic neck, volcanic plug

traits
capped, free-standing, gothic, isolated, jagged, scraggy, solitary

Zuni: "pointed rock," Navajo: *tsé 'íí 'áhí* "standing rock"

knob

battlement, biscuit, bun, buttress, camel hump,
finial, gable, globular sandstone, haystack, mosque,
mudpie, nameless shapes, nipple, nubbin, pancake,
pedestal, pilaster, pillow, pylon, tent rock, tepee,
toadstool, tubercle, turret, turkshead, turtleback,
whaleback, yardang

Scott Milzer, fisherman: *"meadow muffin"*

desert

forms
cold desert, high desert, paleodesert, sage desert,
scrub desert, slickrock desert

arid zone, badlands, barrens, desert floor, desert
mosaic, desert pavement (tessellated), desert varnish
(patina, pitchrock), dry belt, dry solitude, dry zone,
dustbowl (man-made desert), empty quarter, folds,
spare lines, tabula rasa, void, waste, wasteland

traits
ascetic, clean, enduring, painted, prismatic, pure,
spare, spartan

arid, austere, barren, bleak, burnt, colorless, desolate,
desiccated, dried-up, featureless, gutted, meager,
parched, rainless, rock, sere, scant, scorched,
singed, sunbleached, sunstruck, windswept, withered

desierto

Arab: "sand desert"—*erg, sahra,* "stony desert"—
reg (Western Sahara), *serir* (Libya, Egypt), and

hammada; "high desert"—*burr*, Mongol: *gobi*,
Persian: *dasht*, Turk: *kum*

Edward Abbey, writer: *"the tranquil sea of desert,"*
Mary Austin, writer: *"hot sinks of desolation,"* **Honoré
de Balzac**, writer: *"In the desert, there is everything and
there is nothing,"* **Stephen Crane**, writer: *"dull-hued
spaces of mesquite and cactus,"* **Clarence Dutton**, geologist:
"blank, lifeless, and as expressionless as the sea," **Hamlin
Garland**, writer: *"a streamless land,"* **Herman Melville**,
novelist: *"a caked depopulated hell,"* **J. B. Priestley**,
writer: *"brown, bony, sapless, like an old man's hand,"*
Jedediah Smith, mountain man: *"blazing sands"* and
"parched waste," **Owen Wister**, novelist: *"this voiceless
land, this desert, this vacuum,"* **Frank Lloyd Wright**,
architect: *"the abstract land"*

dune

forms
barchan, climbing dune, coppice dune (forms behind
shrub), crescent dune, fossil dune, hanging dune
(falling dune), linear dune, parabolic dune, reversing
dune, seif (longitudinal dune), sidehill dune, star
dune, stellar dune, tail dune, transverse dune

blowsand, comb, dune belt (chain, colony), dune
face, dune line, dunefield, grit, sand cliff, sand
cover, sand drift, sand ripple, sand sheet, sandflow,
sandslide, slip face (leeside), wave

traits
active, attached, fixed, lifeless, live, lunate, shifting,
sinuous, stabilized

Arab: *nefud* "dunefield"

Ralph Bagnold, explorer: *"waves that ought to heave but remained still day after day,"* **Ramson Lomatewama**, poet: *"dry waves of the desert,"* **Wilfred Thesiger**, explorer: *"each dune has its own shape,"* *"whale-backed massifs,"* and *"precipices of sand"*

basin

forms
drainage basin, interior basin, river basin, synclinal basin

blowout (deflation hollow), bowl, caldron, catch-ment, hole, hollow, sandhill bowl, saucer, sink, swag (depression), wallow, weather pit (dry pothole)

bolson "dry basin"

flat

forms
alkali flat, cinder lake, claypan, hardpan, mud flat, pan, sage flat, salt flat, saltpan, sand flat, soda plain, tortilla flat

traits
dry, dead flat, endless, rippled, rock-guarded

mojada "dry lake," *playa*, *salina* "wet playa"

Arab: *sabkha* "salt flat"

Lawrence Durrell, writer: *"flat as a billiard-table"*

arroyo

forms
chute, coulee, cutbank, draw, dry gulch, dry wash,
gulch, gully, rill, sand river, sandwash, storm
sluice, trench, trough, wash

traits
deep-cut, sand-clogged, splayed, u-shaped, v-shaped

hondo "deep arroyo"

Arabian: *wadi*, Australian: water scour

plateau

forms
desert plateau, elevated plain, high plateau, intermontane plateau, summit plain, upcountry, upland

traits
canyon-riven, canyon-shredded, deeply-incised,
deeply-inscribed, deeply-trenched, uplifted

Paiute: "mountain lying down" (plateau)

mesa

forms
altarstone, cathedral rock, mesa escarpment, mesa
wall, mesatop, outlier, platform mountain, pyramid,
erosional remnant, sky island, stepping stone, table,
tabular relief, ziggurat

butte, monument, nipple, temple

___

traits

abrupt, angular, blunt, cliff-bound, colossal, fluted, lava-capped, right-angled, sentinel, sharp-rimmed, square-shouldered, steplike, tabular, terraced

___

Hopi: *tuyqa* "projecting corner of a mesa"

___

mesita "small mesa"

___

Clarence Dutton, geologist: *"bold and striking in outline,"*
D. H. Lawrence, novelist: *"death-grey mesas"*

terrace

___

forms

alluvial terrace (fan terrace), bench, esplanade, rock stairway, story, stream terrace, tier

___

traits

domed, hanging, recessed, shelfy

slickrock

___

forms

baldhead, baldrock, barrens, concave dome, convex rim, curved laminations, curved plane, dunestone, fossil dune, frozen dune, haystack, overlapping lenses, overlapping mounds, petrified dune, pothole garden, sandrock, sandstone billows, slickrock bald, slickrock dome, sliprock, washboard sandstone, whaleback ridge

___

barren, billowy, curvilinear, globular, humpbacked,
humped, lumped, rolling, seamless, slickery,
swirling, twisting, wave-tossed, whorling

crossbedded, cross-stratified, feathered, interbedded,
interfingered, wind-layered

mountain

forms
bastion, chain, crag, dark mass, granitescape, higher
elevations, local relief, massif, montane, mount,
mountain island, mountain mass, mountainside,
orogeny (mountain forming), sky island

basin range, desert range, dry range, lost range,
sawback range

traits
barren, barrier, big-boned, blunt, broken, cloud-
capped, cloud-wrapped, disordered, folded,
guardian, hump-shouldered, ice-scarred, layered,
steeply-pitched, ragged, storm-raked, terraced,
timbered, truncated, weather-cut

cordillera "system of mountain ranges, *sierra*
"sawtooth mountain"

Ivan Doig, novelist: *"weather-making mountains,"* **Gretel
Ehrlich**, writer: *"the horizon bending up on all sides into
mountain ranges,"* **A. B. Guthrie**, novelist: *"wild heights
of rock,"* **D. H. Lawrence**, novelist: *"a tangle of heights,"*
John Reed, journalist: *"rumpled mountains,"* **John Ruskin**,
painter: *"mountain truth"*

peak

___

cleft peak (cloven peak), horn, landmark peak,
pinnacle, relict peak, sawtooth peak, sentinel peak,
snout, spire

___

picacho "sharp peak"

___

demoiselle (slim tower)

summit

___

bald, cone, crest, crown, drum, false summit,
hump, lookout, mountaintop, pulpit, roost, topside

___

Hopi: *oomawki* "cloud house" (summit of San
Francisco Peaks)

___

cumbre or *cima* "summit"

ridge

___

forms
anticlinal ridge, backbone, breaks (badlands), cedar
break (cedar brake—juniper-studded badlands),
couch, crest, cross range, cross-spur, divide, flatiron
(eroded hogback), hogback (sharp crest), interlocking
spurs, leaf, neck, razorback ridge, reef, rib, ridge-
crest, ridgetop, rooster comb, shoulder, spinal
column, spine, spur, spur ridge, talus ridge

___

traits
axial, dividing, knife-edge, horseback, interstream,
monoclinal, pine-laced, offset, saddleback, rock-
ribbed, sawtooth, serrate, splintered, treed, whittled

___

cuesta

___

arête "comb ridge"

John Steinbeck, novelist: *"the sharp snaggled edge of the ridge"*

slope

forms
downslope, facing slope, lee slope, upslope, windward slope

apron, backslope, flank, gradient, gravity slope, heel, hillside, incline, mountainside, pediment (beveled bedrock), pitch, ramp, scree, shoulder, slide (sloping sandstone), slide rock, slip-off slope, talus, talus apron, talus cone, talus slide

alluvial fan (alluvial cone), braided fan, debris fan, gravel fan

traits
fanning, high-angle, incline, responding (opposite), shelving-downward, sparsely-timbered, tilted

bajada "alluvial apron"

hill

forms
cindercone, cinderhill, cone, foothill, hillock, hilltop, hummock, knoll, rise, roll, sandhill, sidehill

traits
conical, crater-shaped, formless, shingled

cerro, cerrito (loma) "small hill"

valley

forms
abandoned valley, anticlinal valley, beaded valley, blind valley, concentric valley, goblet valley (fan—slot—basin), hanging valley, paradoxical valley, racetrack valley (circular), salt valley, strike valley, synclinal valley, transverse valley

bowl, cove, crook, floodplain, flume (deep and narrow), glacial trough, graben (sunken block), hole (mountain-ringed valley), hollow, river bottom, snow bowl, valley floor

traits
box-walled, channel-filled, glaciated, protected, sheltered, wash-braided

pass

break, col (high pass), defile, dip, gap, gate, gunsight, notch, outlet, portal, saddle, sag, wind gap (dry gap, wind gate)

abras "narrow pass," *paso*

ravine

forms
avalanche scar, chine (rocky ravine), chute, couloir, declivity, defile, gash, talus chute, talus ravine

traits
bald, brushy, steep

Michael Paterniti, writer: *"tumble-rock bottom"*

cave

active cave (living, wet), bottomless cave, dead
cave (dry), fault cave, ice cave, slit cave, solution
cave

blowhole, bottomless pit, cavern, earthcrack, grotto,
karst, sink, sinkhole

bacon rind, breakdown, cave pearl, cave popcorn,
column, drapery, dripstone, flowstone, rimstone
pool, stalactite, stalagmite

belly crawl, chamber, crawlway, keyhole passage,
lead, passageway, pit, siphon, well

chupadero "blowhole"

plains

forms
delta plain, desert grassland, high plains, juniper
savanna, long-grass plains, malpais plains, open
range, peneplain, prairie, sagebrush plains, short-
grass plains, steppe, tall grass prairie

traits
bleak, endless, light-filled, open, rolling, unfenced

chaco "grassy alluvial plain," *llano* "dry plain or
high plain"

Wilfred Thesiger, explorer: *"a drab plain, where the wind
spun eddies of dust,"* **Taylor Thompson**, Texas ranger:
"a bald, open prairie"

rock

___

forms
desert pavement, desert varnish (patina, pitchrock), dip, elephant skin (alligator skin), exposure, formation, fretwork, heartrock, houserock, lithic skin, lithosphere (earth's crust), living rock, matrix (ground-mass), mineral soil, native rock (country rock), ore pocket, outcrop, rock plate, rockwork, roughrock, slab, strike, vein, windform

___

alkali bloom, concretion, fulgurite (petrified lightning, lightning-fused), paint stone, pea gravel, petrified wood, ventifact (wind-carved pebble)

___

traits
angular, boxcar-size, broached, calcined, crinkled, crumpled, decayed, decomposed, dense, disintegrated, dissected, etched, frangible (breakable), fatigued, friable (crumbly), granular, hackly, hammered, hewn, impermeable, impervious, jagged, jumbled, lichenous, molded, naked, pitted, porous, pressed, rain-eaten, rain-fluted, rain-washed, rimpled, rotten, rucked, rumpled, seamed, serrated, storm-torn, stressed, sun-heated, sun-shattered, toppled, tumbled, wrinkled, weather-roughened, weather-stained

___

Navajo: "talking rock" (echo forming)

___

Norman Maclean, writer: *"rocks from the basement of time,"* **John McPhee**, writer: *"lithic archive,"* **Henry Miller**, writer: *"This rock is living rock, a divine wave of energy suspended in time and space."*

sedimentary

forms
caliche, claystone, conglomerate, dunestone, evaporite, fossiliferous rock, limestone, mudstone (wrinkled rock), placer, redrock (redstone, redbeds), salt dome, sandstone, searock, shale, siltstone, travertine (calcium carbonate—travertine rim, travertine rind, travertine terrace)

strata

bed, bedding plane, course, horizontals, lamination, laminae, layer, layer cake, page, pancake layering, sheet, shelving, stratification, tablet

traits
entangled, fine-drawn, impervious, mottled, permeable, planar, porous, shattered, stratiform, tabular, tilted, uniform, upended

George Steck, hiker: *"carnivorous limestone,"* **Tony Williams**, traveler: *"the Kaibab crumbles"*

igneous

forms
active volcano, composite volcano (layers of ash, cinder, and lava), dome volcano, dormant volcano, extinct volcano, shield volcano

ash cone, ash flow, basalt, caldera, clinker, columnar jointing, crater, diatreme, dike, ejecta, extrusion, flow, fumarole (vent), intrusion, laccolith, magma, neck, pressure ridge (buckle in flow), pumice, sill, spatter cone, squeeze, tephra, trap rock, tuff, vent, volcanic ash, volcanic bomb, volcanic field, vulcanism

lava

———

aa (rough lava), blister, lava cave, lava cone, lava
dome, lava field, lava flow, pahoehoe (corded lava,
pillow lava, ropy lava), plug, tube

———

Zuni: "fire rock"

———

hornito "spatter mound," *malpais* "volcanic badlands"

———

Arabic: *harra* "lava field"

metamorphic

———

forms
basement rock, gneiss, granite, pegmatite, quartz,
schist, slate

———

traits
adamantine (hard as steel), crustal, pressured, twisted

Eric Newby, writer: *"demoralized granite"*

fossil

---

forms
body fossil, microfossil, trace fossil

---

bone bed, cast, coprolite, fossil bed, fossil quarry, fossil record, fossil remains, gastrolith, mold, ornithopod, paleowind (marks in fossil dunes), ripple rock (water ripples), sauropod, scute (armor plate)

---

traits
articulated, disarticulated, exploded, extinct

Scott Madsen, paleontologist: *"blue bone" and "fool's bone,"* **Scott Milzer**, fisherman: *"bigmacasuarus," "humungasaurus," and "outasightasaurus"*

trackway

---

burrow, claw mark, footprint, gait, impression, imprint, pad, print, running gait, track, track-bearing bed, trackmaker, tracksite, trail

meteoric

---

falling star, fireball (large meteorite), impact crater, impact feature, leonid shower, meteoric dust, meteor shower, meteor swarm, meteor train, meteor trail, meteorite, shatter cone

movement

—

fold

—

forms
anticline, buckle, chevron fold, crustal fold, down-warp, flex, flexure, monocline, swell, syncline, upwarp, warp

—

traits
arched, contorted, creased, crimped, wrenched

fault

—

forms
downthrow, downthrust, overthrust fault, reverse fault, slickensides (polished surface along fault), throw, upthrow, upthrust

—

traits
dead, downthrown, parallel, upthrown

earthquake

—

aftershock, epicenter, liquifaction, quake, seismic wave, shatter belt, shave wave (shear wave, transverse wave), tremblor, tremor, tsunami

erosion

—

forms
aeolian (eolian) erosion, biological erosion, fluvial erosion, headward erosion, lateral erosion, sheet erosion

—

cycles of erosion, debris, detritus, erosion scar, erosional remnant, exfoliation, fill, frost-shattering, frost-wedging, landslide, landslip, mass wasting, piping (badlands erosion), plant wedging, residual boulder (weathered in place), retreating cliff, rill network, rockfall, rockslide, rock glacier, rubble, sediment, spall, slump block, slumping, stream piracy (beheading, capture), talus, unconformity, vestige

---

differential weathering, selective weathering, shadow weathering

---

traits
fractal, streamlined, time-worn, trenched, waterworn, wind-worn, worked and reworked

---

motion
abrade, batter, downcut, chisel, chop, cleave, cross-cut, etch, furrow, gouge, grind, gully, incise, line, pockmark, polish, press, pulverize, rake, rill, rip, sandblast, score, scour, scrub, scrumble, sculpt, slump, strip, sunder, weather, topple, trench, tumble, undercut, undermine (sap), whittle

---

Herbert Gregory, geologist: *"piled in confusion"* and *"headward gnawing,"* **Tom Lea**, writer: *"ancient crumblings, dry scourings"*

SKY

day

forms

the blue, broad daylight, colorless noon, dayside,
face of the sky, envelope of air, firmament, living
air, meridian, meridian passage (transit), noonday
sky, noonday sun, patch, perpendicular sun,
skyscape, sucker hole, sunflash, upper hemisphere,
vault, visible air, visible sky, western sky, winter
sky, winter sun, zenith

traits

ancient, auroral, bracing, clear-cut, cloudbound,
cloudless, domed, empty, everblue, flaring, funereal,
glass-clear, high, hollow, leadening, lowering,
nubilous (cloudy), ocean-blue, opaque, overcast,
paint-blue, rain-washed, remote, severe, slate, soft,
stainless, stereoscopic, sunshot, thin, torn

Hopi: *tawávi'a* (opaque image of sun visible
through intervening clouds), Navajo: "horizontal
blue," Ute: *takoop-pa*, "earth cover"

Reyner Banham, writer: *"high, staring light,"* **Forrest
Carter**, writer: *"vast, bending sky,"* **William Gass**, novelist:

"the sky's pale deep endlessness," **D. H. Lawrence**, novelist: *"high-up day,"* **Haniel Long**, writer: *"the terrible sun,"* **Pierre Loti**, traveler: *"a sky so high above that it can be forgotten,"* **Harvey Mudd**, poet: *"rake of low sun,"* **Jedediah Smith**, mountain man: *"floods of light,"* **John Steinbeck**, novelist: *"The sky was brushed clean by the wind."*

dawn

breaking light, dawnlight, daybreak, false dawn, first light, halflight, sunrise, sunup

Hopi: purple dawn (can see shape of man), yellow dawn (can see man's breath), red sunrise (can see full man), Navajo: "light misted up" and "horizontal white"

T. Coraghessan Boyle, novelist: *"chill light of dawn,"* **Dante**, poet: *"widening dawn"* and *"the holy hour,"* **Hamlin Garland**, writer: *"flare of horizontal heat,"* **Cormac McCarthy**, novelist: *"rumors of light,"* **Frank Waters**, writer: *"The whole vast land rose shudderingly."*

light

forms
airlight (blue veil), ambient light, available light, bounce light, cathedral light, dead light, dispersed light, emitted light, envelope of light, firelight, halflight, highlight, incoming light, light passage, light path, light space, light wave, side light, specular light, visible light

backlighting, backscattering (eyeshine), blaze, brilliance, column, curtain, dayglow, field, filament, fluorescence, flush, glare, gleam, glint, grain,

halftone, illumination, incandescence, iridescence,
jet of sunlight, layer of transparence, luminosity,
luster, nimbus (aura, glow), path, radiance,
refraction, startling clarity, self-luminous, shaft,
spark, sheen, sunshine, vein, wave

corona (ring around sun seen through thin clouds),
green flash, solar pillar (shaft above rising/setting
sun), streamer, sundog (perihelia, mock sun,
weather dog)

desert mirage, false pond, fata morgana, highway
mirage, inferior mirage, spirit lake, superior mirage

traits
amber, ancient, bland, bleaching, blinding, blistering,
bright, clear, consuming, crystalline, dead, dim,
dusty, dry, effulgent (shining brilliantly), emitted,
endless, enveloping, eternal, ethereal, fading,
falling, fluid, full, grainy, harsh, incoming, latent,
long-traveled, living, low-angled, lucent, lucid,
luminous, pervasive, measureless, momentary,
natural, numinous, oblique, preternatural, quivering,
radiant, rarefied, revealing, saturating, searing,
sliding (low-angle), soft, solid, subdued, sudden,
sunflexed, suspended, textured, tonal, transforming,
trapped, true, twice-reflected, unbroken, vibratory,
visible, weak, wide, zodiacal

motion
bore, bounce, burn, burnish, burst, deflect, diffract,
diffuse, dissolve, drain, drive, explode, flare, flicker,
flood, glance, glaze, glow, hammer, interplay, irradiate,
kindle, paint, penetrate, poke, pulse, radiate, rain,
reflect, refract, saturate, scatter, shed, shoot, sift,
slice, spangle, splash, stream, strike, suffuse, waver

Hopi: *siitalawva* "flower light" (landscape bright with flowers after a rain)

Ganzfeld (directionless, suspended color field)

Reyner Banham, writer: *"color-eating light,"* **Bruce Berger**, writer: *"a directionless radiance,"* **Dante**, poet: *"infected light,"* **Guy Davenport**, essayist: *"January light,"* **Clarence Dutton**, geologist: *"the metallic glare of the haze"* and *"Rembrandt lights,"* **Johann Wolfgang von Goethe**, philosopher: *"migration of light,"* **Joseph Joubert**, writer: *"waves of light and layers of brightness,"* **Tom Lea**, writer: *"empty glare,"* **John Sargent**, painter: *"captured light,"* **Simon Schama**, writer: *"facets of light,"* **Henry David Thoreau**, writer: *"a great awakening light,"* **Vincent Van Gogh**, painter: *"tempered light"*

color

forms
foundation color, fugitive color, local color, raw color

cast, chromatic field, coloration, color mass, complimentary vibration, degree, density, desert monochrome, dusky (dim, shadowy), earth tone, effusion, endless hues, fluid pigment, flush, gradation, grade, hue, paint, pallor, pigment, pinto, scale, shade, shiller (iridescent luster), spectrum, splash, stain, tinge, tint, tone, value, wash, wave

traits
acidic, bleached, burning, chalky, chromatic, dead, drab, dull, dusty, faint, florid, healing, hidden, incandescent, iridescent, lackluster, latent, luminous, matte, mottled, multihued, mute, nameless, opaque, pale, pastel, pallid, penetrating, primal, prismatic,

relentless, self-vibrant, sharp, spectral, stale, stippled, subdued, tactile, thermal, transcendent, translucent, transparent, untamed, variegated, vibratory, withering

Paul Cézanne, painter: *"The colours of things rise up from the roots of the earth,"* **Kenneth Clark**, scholar: *"web of pure color"* and *"broken touches of pure color,"* **Colin Fletcher**, writer: *"a fusion of colors,"* **Pierre Loti**, traveler: *"neutral tones of nothing at all,"* **Vladimir Nabokov**, novelist: *"unruly colors of the universe,"* **John Ruskin**, painter: *"a mass of color,"* **Terry Tempest Williams**, writer: *"the spectrum of stones"*

red

bloodred, carmine (purplish red), cayenne, cinnabar, clay red, crimson, flaming red, Ganado red, heliotrope (reddish purple), hematite, henna (light red), monotone red, red ocher (ochre), rust red, terra cotta (brownish red), vermilion (fiery red)

colorado "reddish," *vermejo* "auburn"

Maynard Dixon, painter: *"canyon red"*

blue

ash blue, cathedral blue, china blue, close blue, flawless blue, horizon blue, mountain blue, night blue, pure spectral blue, raw blue, resolute blue, salty blue, skyblue, smoke blue, solid blue, Taos blue, transparent blue, utter blue

James Galvin, writer: *"a willing blue"*

green

bottle green, living green, new green, sage, slate green, sour green, spring green, sulfurous green, viridian (blue-green)

yellow

acid yellow, claybank (dull, brownish yellow), dry mustard, lemon, parchment yellow, sandstone yellow, tawny (brownish yellow), yellow ocher

orange

blaze orange, hunter orange, safety orange

brown

buff (color of tanned buffalo skin), burnt umber (reddish brown), cedar brown, dun (grayish brown, dust-colored), earthtone, henna (reddish brown), khaki, nut brown, raw umber (yellowish brown), russet (reddish brown), sand, sawdust brown, tobacco brown

gray

ash gray, chalk gray, cool gray, dead gray, halftone grays, leaden gray, nickel gray, smoke gray

black

manganese black, metallic black, raven black, starless black

white

blank white, bone white, cranial white, crystal white, dead white, elemental white, full-moon white, lunar white, Navajo white

tierra blanca "austere off-white"

cloud

forms
banner cloud, cauliflower cloud (cumulus), drift-cloud, fair-weather cloud, heap cloud, layer cloud, lenticular cloud (windblown), stormcloud, thunder-cap, thundercloud, thunderhead, wave cloud

cirrus (horsetails, mare's tails), cirrocumulus (mackerel sky, rippling), cirrostratus (halo around sun or moon), altocumulus (woolly), cumulonimbus (anvilhead), altostratus (high, gray sheet), strato-cumulus (bumpy, rolls), nimbostratus (rain-bearing), nimbus (rain-bearing), cumulus (flat-based, dome-shaped, short-lived), stratus (overcast, low ceiling)

clag (low-hanging, shredded cloud), cloudburst (swirling cloud formation), cloud deck, cloud mass, cloudscape, cloud slope, crown, puff, rack (cloud-mass driven before wind), rim of clouds, scud (low, dark clouds moving quickly), shelf, smear, streamer, surf, tuft, veil, wave, wisp, wrack

fog, fogpatch, frontal fog, ground fog, mist, pea-soup fog

California: tule fog

Paiute: *pogonip* "frozen winter mist"

traits

anvil-headed, bulbous, filmy, flying, globular,
hanging, low-lying, massed, mountainous, patchy,
ragged (fractus), restless, ribbed, shredded, stratified,
tattered, thready, torn, translucent, uneasy,
unraveling, wavy, wind-driven

———

motion

billow, boil, cling, drift, float, fly, fold, hang, heap,
hover, pile, roil, roll, scud, seethe, smolder, spill,
spread, stack, stretch, swell, swirl, tumble, unfurl,
whirl

———

Hopi: *oomaotu* "rainclouds" and *tala'omaw*
"summer cloud"

———

Edward Abbey, writer: *"dense as wool,"* **Charles Baudelaire**, poet: *"cloud-disheveled air,"* **Eric Newby**, writer: *"vast mushroom-shaped clouds,"* **Job**, patriarch: *"the spreading of the clouds"*

shadow

forms
cloud rays (shafts of shadow), falloff (change from shadow to light), penumbra, pool of shade, lost edges (within shadow), shadowline, umbra

traits
attached, barred, blue, clear-cut, crisp, deep, hollow, massing, sharp-edged, somber, thrown

night

___

forms
airglow (nightglow), blank night, blue desert
darkness, dry darkness, evening face, nightside,
planetary dark, scotopia (eye's ability to adjust to
darkness), shrouded regions of space, starless air,
true dark, visual grays

___

traits
blanketing, bristling, concealing, deep, enveloping,
impenetrable, naked, pitch dark, shot with stars,
shrouded, star-strewn, starlit, transparent

___

Navajo: "rolling darkness"

___

Edward Dahlberg, poet: *"primeval night,"* **Vaclav Havel**,
poet statesman: *"a realm of darkness,"* **Cormac McCarthy**,
novelist: *"absolute night,"* **John Milton**, poet: *"the hollow
dark"* and *"ancient night,"* **Thomas Wolfe**, novelist:
"the far dark"

dusk

___

afterglow, alpenglow, darkfall, diminishing day,
failing light, fallen sun, firestorm sunset, gathering
darkness, halflight, last light, near darkness, night-
fall, sundown, twilight, twilight arch (red-blue
band leading night across the sky), vanishing day

___

Navajo: "horizontal yellow"

___

Edward Abbey, writer: *"the chemistry of twilight,"* **Mary
Austin**, writer: *"the twilight tide,"* **Robert Duncan**, poet:
"the dying down of the light," **Richard Grossinger**, writer:
"dark ecotone of twilight," **A.B. Guthrie**, novelist: *"dark
drifting down," "darkness crowding in"* and *"the long*

western sun," **Barry Lopez**, writer: *"the slow inhalation of light,"* **Cormac McCarthy**, novelist: *"sudden rush of dark,"* **John Reed**, journalist: *"the passing of the light,"* **Jim Turrell**, artist: *"nightrise"*

moon

___

forms
crescent moon, first half moon, full moon, half-disk moon, harvest moon, hunter's moon (first full moon after harvest moon), new moon, old moon, paleolithic moon, quarter moon, second half moon, waning moon (old crescent moon), waxing moon (new crescent moon, young crescent moon)

___

cusp, dark phase, dark side (backside, far side), darkened disk, disk (disc), full moonrise (flat, gibbous, oblate, swollen), horns, lunar rhythm, moonrise, moonset, orb, rind, sliver

___

traits
calendric, conchoid (semicircular), flat, half-hidden, half-illuminated, half-revealed, hemispheric, lunar, lunate, sharp, sterile, wasted, windless

___

motion
float, hover, lift, set, sink

___

Texas: Comanche moon (September full moon)

star

___

constellation, darkstar, dawnstar, evening star, galaxy, maze of stars, morning star, points of light, polestar, star cloud, star drift, starfield, starlight, starshine, star stream

___

traits
astral, burning, cold, drifting, faint, innumerable, revolving, scintillating, stellar, turning, twinkling, unseen

___

Tohono O'odham: "magician's daughter" (morning star)

___

Michael Disney, writer: *"pale archway of light" (Milky Way),*
John Steinbeck, novelist: *"stars stabbing and sharp"*

weather

___

forms
heavy weather, local weather, mountain weather

___

air mass, cold front, fair skies, high pressure ridge, inversion, occluded front, microclimate, unstable air mass, upper-air turbulence, warm front, weather-edge

___

traits
deteriorating, mercurial, pea-soup, savage, stark, wild

___

Tyler Williams, river guide: *"wrap-around weather"*

storm

___

forms
eye, foot, hailstorm, ice storm, leading edge, rain-storm, squall, squall line, storm cell, storm front, storm path, storm track, storm train, thick of storm, training (stormcells arriving in quick succession), windstorm

___

cyclone, funnel cloud, tornado, twister

___

traits
brewing, dissipating, electric, flash, galvanic, sudden

motion
build, decay, hit, slam

Taklimakan Desert: *kara-buran* "black storm"

C. L. Rawlins, writer: *"a blue-dark roll of storm"*

lightning

forms
ball lightning, beaded lightning (chain, channel, pearl), blind lightning, branched lightning, crown flash, dry lightning, flash lightning, forked lightning, forked-channel lightning, ground flash, heat lightning (sheet lightning, summer lightning), ribbon lightning (rapid strikes pushed sideways by the wind)

traits
dry, jagged, shearing, tortuous, zigzag

motion
blast, bolt, flash, flicker, plunge, pulse, streak, strike, stroke, surge

Jack Kerouac, novelist: *"dense, electric air,"* **Barry Lopez**, writer: *"a white-lightning sky,"* **Cormac McCarthy**, novelist: *"silent lightning flaring sheetwise"*

thunder

forms
thunder boomer, thunderbolt, thunderclap

traits
crashing, distant, dry, dull, muted, prolonged,
rattling, rolling, rumbling

sounds
boom (distant), clap, clash, crack (nearby), crash,
explode, fire, peal, profound rumble, rattle,
reverberate, rip, roll, rumble, volley

Navajo: "blue thunder" and "dark thunder"

stormlight

broken light, crepuscular rays (twilight), lightray,
sunburst, sunray, sunshaft

Jay Dusard, photographer: *"Jesus light,"* **Clarence Dutton**,
geologist: *"glory-rifts,"* **Michael Melford**, photographer:
"Arizona light"

rain

forms
baptism of rain, deluge, dollops, downpour, gully
washer, infall, monsoon, rain cell, rain column,
rain curtain, rain streamer, raindrop, rainfall, rain-
veil, rainwash, serein (fine, evening rain falling
from apparently clear sky), shower, shreds, smirr
(drizzle), spatter, squall, tendrils, torrent, wisps

traits
cascading, drenching, driving, flamadiddle beat
(hail), flooding, glistening, incessant, lacerating,
pluvial, pelting, pounding, quenching, sheeting,
soaking, spasmodic, sudden, trailing, torrential,
violent

motion
clouds unload, patter, slap, splatter, sluice down

Navajo: "dark rain," "rainray," and "streaked rain"

chubasco "cloudburst," *equipatas* "light winter rain," Sonora: *las aguas* "summer rains"

Bashō, poet: *"smoky rain,"* **Jim Griffith**, folklorist: *"toad-strangler,"* **Elizabeth Simpson**, writer: *"visible rain,"* **Rabindranath Tagore**, poet: *"the madly rushing rain."*

dry rain

fallstreaks, ghost rain, precipitation trails, short fall, streamers, virga

Hopi: "standing rain"

rainbow

Alexander's dark bow (band between double bow), double bow, fogbow (cloudbow), mistbow (primary and secondary), moonbow (lunarbow)

mud

boghole, gumbo, mud cracks, mud curls, oozehole, quicksand, sinkhole, slowsand

Bob Dye, river guide: *"jiggle mud,"* **Peter Watts**, writer: *"cricksand"*

wind

forms

basin wind, contrary wind, cross wind, dominant
wind, downcanyon wind, head wind, catabolic
wind (drainage wind, gravity wind, valley wind),
local wind, mountain crest wind, mountain wind,
peak winds, nightwind, planetary winds, polar
wind, prevailing wind, stowed wind (concentrated
in pass), tail wind, thaw wind, upcanyon wind

air mass, airflow, airstream, blow, blue screamer,
blurbles (turbulence over ridges), breath, breeze,
current, downdraft (air fall, fall wind, downburst),
downwind, draft, eddy, evening blow, flaw (sudden
gust), gale, gust, gust front, inflow, inrush, jetstream,
lee side, leeward, light air (slight breeze), microburst,
restless air, tracery of wind, thermal, turbulence,
updraft, upwind, vortex, westerlies, wind eddy
(lee wave), wind shear, windblast, windage, wind-
stream, windward

California: Santa Ana (blows down coastal canyons),
chubasco (off-coast squall from the south); Rocky
Mountain and Northwest: chinook (snow-eater)
and williwaw (cold blast off the coastal range),
Sonora: *norte*, *papagayo* "norther," Texas: blue
norther (bitter north wind), blue whistler, Cayuse
wind, cow skinner

traits

abrasive, arid, blustery, burning, choking, cutting,
desiccating, depleted, driving, drying, dust-laden,
erratic, gale force, high-velocity, keening, moaning,
overheated, piercing, rain-bearing, raw, sand-driving,
savage, shearing, squirrely, steady, stiff, superheated,
unrelenting, vagrant, westerly

motion

blast, bluster, buffet, build, burnish, cut, eddy, fan,
fret, grind, rake, rasp, riffle, scour, shake, shift,
slam, spill, spin, sweep, swirl, tear, veer, waft, wail,
whip, whirl, whorl

_____

die, lull, shrivel, subside, taper off

_____

Hopi: *kwingyaw* "northwind" (ice cold, malevolent)
and "wind road," Navajo: "blue wind," "dark wind,"
"rolling wind," "slender wind," "wind standing
within," "wind that drives up a rain," and "wind
that stirs the dust"

_____

Arabic: *haboob* "violent wind"

_____

Bashō, poet: *"cloud-moving wind," "the sore wind,"*
and "the roar of pine trees upon distant mountains,"
William Kittredge, writer: *"buckaroo wind,"*
C. L. Rawlins, writer: *"gust-front"*

sandstorm

_____

black blizzard, black roller, dry haze, dry storm,
duststorm, duster, dust-up, roller, sandblast

_____

Arizona cloudburst, Texas rain

dust devil

_____

dancing devil, dust twister, dust whirl, dustspout,
sand auger, sand spout, sandwhirl, whirligig,
whirlwind

_____

Navajo: "coiled wind"

_____

tornillo

dust

___

alkali dust, dust cloud, dust pocket, dustwell, puff, rock dust

___

Hopi: *qö'angw* "dust raised by the wind," Navajo: "falling dust," "fringed dust," and "rolling dust"

___

Bill Hatcher, photographer: *"moon dust" (powdery dust)*

stillness

___

forms
empty time, envelope of silence, eye of the storm, heart of silence, hush, lull, mute, silence encased, suspension of time, untroubled air, vast silence, windless air, windstill

___

traits
absolute, charged, pervading, profound, utter

___

Kenneth Clark, scholar: *"lunar silence," **Oakley Hall**,* writer: *"galvanic stillness," **D. H. Lawrence**,* novelist: *"fierce silence," **John McPhee**,* writer: *"great spatial silence," **Everett Ruess**,* artist: *"ominous, murky calm," **Frank Waters**: "insupportable silence"*

heat

___

forms
cauldron, dead heat, fluid tremor of heat, furnace, heat wave, scorcher, sizzler

___

traits
baking, blistering, choking, deadening, drowsy, dry, enervating, fluid, glassy, leveling, oppressive, reflector-oven, scalding, searing, shimmering,

sizzling, soporific, stifling, stupefying, thick, torrid,
undulating, wavering, white

_____

Leo Banks, journalist: *"hot enough to bend spoons"*

drought

_____

forms
bone dry, dry spell, flat heat haze, the big dry

_____

traits
desiccating, hyperarid, parched, xeric

_____

Wallace Ott, rancher: *"awful drouthy"*

cold

_____

forms
cold drainage (cold sink, cold trap, frost pocket),
cold snap, cold spell, dank (moist and chilly),
freezing point, freeze-up, frigid, wind chill, zero
weather

_____

traits
arctic, bitter, brittle, crisp, numbing, polar, sharp

snow

_____

forms
corn snow, drift snow, red snow (pink snow,
watermelon snow), spring snow

_____

blizzard, diamond dust (crystals floating in clear,
cold air), graupel (pellets, snow crystals coated
with rime, soft hail), ground blizzard, skiff, snow-
fall, snowflake, whiteout

_____

blanket, cornice, firn (firnspiegel—snow surviving
the spring thaw), meltwater crust, powder, rolling
swells, sastrugi (carved into waves), scour hole
(wind eddy behind a rock or tree), snow bank,
snowdrift, suncrust, suncup, snowfield, snowline,
snowpack, windcrust, wind etching, wind loading

glaze, glint, sparkle

traits
branch-breaking, crystalline, dead, driving, goose-
down, rotten, settled, wild

Navajo: "on-the-branch snow" (sticks to branches),
"horse-tracks snow" (so thin hoofs expose bare
ground), "inlaw chaser" (big snowstorm with
heavy, dark clouds)

Aristophanes, playwright: *"the snow peppered down"*

avalanche

forms
ice avalanche, loose-slab avalanche, slab avalanche,
sluff, snowslide, spindrift, wind-slab avalanche

avalanche hazard, avalanche path, avalanche scar,
avalanche terrain, avalanche track, avalanche trigger,
avalanche wind

cone, fracture line, runout zone, suspect slope,
trigger point

motion
release, roar, run, settle (whumph), sluff

ice

___

black frost (blackens leaves), black ice, film, frost
haze, frost heave, frost nipped, frozen rain, glaze
ice, hail, hailstone, hard frost, ice dust, ice fog,
ice sand, ice shelf, ice wedge, killing frost, rime
(dull surface, deposited on windward side), sleet

___

depth hoar (sugar snow), hoarfrost (cold-weather
dew, fern frost, hoar thorns, ice grass, window
frost), surface hoar

___

George Renner, cedar chestmaker: *"frozen in their tracks"*

glacier

___

forms
active glacier, alpine glacier, continental glacier,
hanging glacier, lateral glacier, mountain glacier,
passive glacier, retreating glacier, terminal glacier,
tributary glacier, valley glacier

___

crevasse, boulder field, cirque, drift, drumlin,
erratic, esker, firn line (where snow never melts),
glacial breeze, glaciation, ice bridge, icecap, icefall,
icefield, kame, kettle, kettlehole, meltwater lake,
moulin (ice well, millwell), outwash plain,
periglacial, pressure ridge (ogives), rock flour (glacial
silt), serac (ice tower), snout, till, toe, tongue

___

lateral moraine, medial moraine, recessional
moraine, terminal moraine

___

motion
advance, calve, carve, grind, inch, retreat

WATER

flowing water

___

forms

drainage, dribble, episodic runoff, filament, film,
flume, fluvial runoff, inflow, mainstream, meltwater,
outflow, oxbow (meander bow), peak flow, rainwash,
rill, rivulet, run, runnel, runoff, scourline, sheetwash,
snowmelt, spillway, spume, steep creek, streamlet,
streamway, thread, torrent, trace, track, vein, water-
course, waterline, watershed, waterway

___

artery, arm, barbed tributary (points upstream),
branch, feeder, fork, lateral stream, principle
tributary, prong, stringer, tributary, tributary creek

___

bore, debris flow, flash flood, flood stage, floodflow,
mud flow, sheet flood, spate (sudden flood)

river

___

forms

antecedent river, countersunk river, ephemeral
river (intermittent river, perennial river, seasonal
river), inflowing river

___

backwater, canyon-cutter, channel, downstream,
fall line, fastwater, flatwater, gradient, headwaters,
mainstream, midstream, mouth, pleat (right-angle
turn of river), rivercourse, river profile, source,
upstream

backflow, confluence, conflux, converging currents
(seam), crosscurrent, downstream current, main
current, upstream current

disappearing river, dry river, forgotten river, hidden
river, lost river, upside-down river, sinking river,
sunken river

traits
aerated, agitated, braided, chili-colored, confluent,
constricted, convulsive, curly, dendritic, entrenched,
flashing, fluvial, frayed, gypy, life-giving, living,
lothic (rapidly-flowing), murmuring, navigable,
perennial, quarrying, rare, riffling, rippling, ruffling,
sleek, slick, sluggish, spreading, storm-fed, sunken,
swollen, tangled, tossing, turbulent, turgid,
unreachable, vascular

motion
blow, careen, career, churn, collect, course, crank,
curl, dart, discharge, drift, empty, feed, flash, float,
flow, flush, gurgle, gush, lap, lick, meander, outpour,
part, percolate, plunge, ramp, recede, rise, roil,
roll, rush, seethe, shoot, slide, sluice, speed, splice,
spread, stream, surge, swash, swirl, thread, trickle,
uprush, upwell, wend

Karok: *káruk* "upriver," Navajo: *bits'íís ninéézi*
"river of never-ending life" (Colorado)

rio, rillito "little river or stream"

Black Elk, holy man: *"fearful dark river,"* **Clarence Dutton**, geologist: *"a headlong torrent foaming and plunging over rocky rapids,"* **James Joyce**, novelist: *"riverrun, past Eve & Adam's,"* **Eric Newby**, writer: *"the whirring of hidden streams,"* **Ezra Pound**, poet: *"the underwave,"* **John Wesley Powell**, explorer: *"this solemn, mysterious way,"* **John Vernon**, novelist: *"sliding plane of water"*

riverside

bank, beach, berm (deposit at the top of a beach), brookbed, cutbank, delta, embankment, river left, river right, riverbank, riverbed, sandbank, sandbar

rapids

forms
backwash, boil, boil line, boulder garden, broken water, burble line (blurble line, bubble line), chute, eddy, eddy fence, eddyline, fastwater, fretwater, hole, hydraulic jump, hydraulics, keeper, logjam, reversal, riffle, slackwater, sleeper, sousehole, spirtle, stopper, strainer, sweeper, tongue, vortex, wash cycle, washback hole, whirlpool (suckie), whitewater

backcurling wave (backcresting wave, backroller), compression wave, crest, curler, domer, haystack, herringbone wave, lateral wave, pillow, ripple, roller, roostertail, sand wave, side curler, standing wave, swirlie, tailwave, traveling wave, V-wave, wave train

traits
churning, doable, dull roar, erupting, explosive, freight-train fast, heavy, grinding, percussive, runable, spitting, undulating, unrunable

motion
billow, buck, catapult, chug, crash, kick, pitch and
roll, pound, pump, surge, tangle, tumble

John Wesley Powell, explorer: *"mad waters"* and *"the
roaring fall,"* *Wallace Stegner*, writer: *"wild pile-up
of water,"* *John Vernon*: *"hanging avalanche of water"*

waterfall

cascade, cataract, falls, overfall, plunge basin,
plunge pool, pouroff, pourover, rimfall, sheeted
waterfall, tricklefalls

spring

dripping spring, ephemeral seep, fault-line spring,
gyp spring (alkaline), headspring, intermittent spring,
perennial spring, seasonal spring, seep, seepage,
soda spring, wet-weather seep

Sonora: *nacimiento* "place where water is born,"
ojo, sumidero "hidden spring"

Australian: "soak" (dugout seep)

hydrothermal

forms
cone, crater, eruptive phase, fumarole (steam vent),
geyser field, geyserite (sinter), hot pool (thermal pool),
mud pot (paint pot), overflow, perpetual spouter,
pre-eruptive splash (preplay), run-off channel,
spouter, steam phase, thermal basin, thermal fog,
travertine (rind, drapery), underground plumbing

active geyser, cone geyser, dormant geyser, extinct geyser, fountain geyser, subordinate geyser

___

boiling spring, hot spring, hydrothermal spring, thermal spring, warm spring

___

motion
bubble, eject, erupt, gurgle, hiss, jet, splash, sputter

standing water

___

aquifer, bitter lake, crater lake, dead zone (bathtub ring—mineral stain around reservoir), deadwater, fossil water, groundwater, inlet, oxbow lake, perched water table, salt lake, tarn (small mountain lake often in a cirque), turnover (seasonal mixing of lakewater), water table

___

bedrock pool, catch basin, coyote well, ephemeral pool, pothole, plunge pool, rain apron, rainpocket, rainpool, rock pool, trap, travertine pool, waterhole, wateringhole, waterpan, waterpocket, weathering pit

___

cattle tank, guzzler, rainwater tank, stock tank, trick tank

___

alberca "waterhole," *charco* "puddle," *hueco* "rainwater basin," *laguna, playa* "ephemeral lake," *pozo* "well or shallow pool," *salina* "salty playa or spring," *tanque, tinaja* "waterhole"

___

Australia: billabong "dead river" (oxbow lake)

___

Hopi: *paahu* "waterhole"

___

Charles Bowden, writer: *"the hidden waters,"* **Harvey Butchart**, hiker: *"pollywog soup"* (waterhole)

FIRE

---

forms

backcountry fire, backfire, brushfire, crown fire,
forest fire, grass fire, high-intensity fire, lightning
fire, low-intensity fire, natural fire, plume fire,
ridge fire, spot fire, wildfire, wildland fire

---

blaze, blowup, brand, burn pattern (fire mosaic),
burnt land, charred zone, cinder, combustion, crest,
ember, firebrand, flame, flame-sheet, heat chimney,
heat stress (trees), hot spot, slop-over (jumps fireline),
spark, stream, tongue, underburn, wall, wave

---

caldron, conflagration, firestorm, holocaust, inferno,
maelstrom, whirlwind of fire

---

broadcast burn, controlled burn (light burn,
management burn, prescribed burn), epic burn

---

traits

blistering, crackling, deadly, devastating,
incandescent, leaping, searing, stiff, superheated,
suppressible, unchecked, voracious, wind-driven

---

motion
arc, blast, burn, char, climb, combust, consume,
creep, crown, curl, drive, eat, erupt, explode, fan,
flare up, flicker, funnel, gallop, hit, hopscotch,
ignite, incinerate, jump, lick, outflank, overrun,
push, race, rage, rampage, rip, roar, roast, run, skip,
smolder, shower (sparks), spray (sparks), spread,
storm, surge, sweep, swell, swirl, threaten, torch,
whip

sound
deafening roar, hiss, roar, rumble, woof

Brad Haugh, Storm King Fire survivor: *"a tornado
on fire,"* **Elers Koch,** forest ranger: *"fire breeds fire"*
and *"the very air was on fire"*

smoke

forms
billow, cloud, column, curtain, dead smoke, drift
smoke, haze, pall, plume, smoke trail, taint, tang

traits
acrid, boiling, choking, dense, moiling, resinous,
suffocating

motion
billow, boil, choke, drift, enshroud, mushroom,
rush, tower, twist, wreathe

LIFE

habitat

---

biome, biotic province, corridor (dispersal route),
ecological island, ecological gradient, ecosystem,
lifezone, microclimatic zone, microhabitat,
refugium, riparian (riverside)

---

brulé (burnt-wood), cactus forest, catclaw thicket,
cedar glade, climax forest, desertscrub, doghair pine
(haired up, a thick stunted stand), hanging garden
(alcove garden, terrace garden), jungle (mesquite
thicket of Southwest Texas), motte (clump of trees),
muskeg, oasis, old-growth forest, park, piñon-juniper
woodland (dwarf forest, p-j, pygmy forest), forest
mantle, mountain grassland, spire forest, subalpine,
swale, timberland, treeline (upper and lower), tundra,
yellow pine forest (ponderosa)

---

alamo "cottonwood," *bosque* "grove near water,
woodland, or thick mesquite stand," *brasada*
"brushcountry" (Texas), *chaparral* "scrub oak thicket,"
cienega "wet meadowlands," *encinal* (encino)
"oakwood," *fresno* "ash tree," *mesquital* "mesquite
woodland," *monte* "hillside scrub," *portrero*

"pastureland or tongue of high ground," *sabino* "juniper," *vega* "open, watered grassland"

plant

annual, buckbrush, flag tree (branches stripped on the windward side), perennial, quakie (aspen), rank growth, scrag (thin, stunted tree), spindly brush, straggling brush, stubby pine (pinyon), Spanish bayonet (yucca), subnivean (plants under snow), succulent (thick, fleshy leaves), treetop, tussock, underbrush, undergrowth, windfall (deadfall, jack-straw downfall, windsnap, windthrow), witness tree, xeric

Taylor Thompson, Texas ranger: *"a skirting of timber"*

leaf

blade, leaf mosaic (leaf arrangement maximizing sunlight), leafstalk, midrib, vein

animal

browser, elk (wapiti), gallery (tracks of beetle larvae in the bark), Gila monster (beaded lizard), grazer, home range, horned lizard (horny toad), marmot (rock chuck, whistle pig), mule deer (mulie, stot—to leap and land on all four legs), predator, prey, pronghorn (antelope)

Navajo: lizard "little cousin to the snake"

Australian: thorny devil (horny toad)

coat
guard hairs (coarse), scut (short, stumpy tail), scute (horny plates—lizards), underfur (fine), underhair

sound
rattlesnake (buzzworm): buzzing rattle, whirr

coyote (songdog): mad bark, quavering cry, ululation, wavering howl, yelp, yip

canyon treefrog: Buck Crowley, kayaker: "croak like a hoarse goat"

cicada: chirr, electric buzz, harsh trill, shrill whine

horned lizard (horny toad): open-mouth hiss

elk: bugle "sounds like it's passing a kidney stone"

bird

----

hummer, raptor, songbird

----

motion
aerial acrobatics, barrel roll, dart, dive, effortless
glide, flap, flip, flit, float, glide, gyral path, halfturn,
hang in the air, lazy figure-eight, lazy swing, lift,
phantom-like glide, pivot, plummet, prey drop,
reel, roll, sail, slip, soar, stall, suspend, swing,
swoop, tumble, veer and turn, wheel, wobbly drift

----

sound
redtail hawk: "keeeeer keeer," "kee-ahrr," screak,
scream, screech, skee

canyon wren: cadenza, clear song, falling scale, liquid
trilling, spiraling call, "tee-tee-tee-teer teer teer"

Larry Stevens, biologist: *"clear, descending whistle"*
(canyon wren)

mourning dove: plaintive call

trogon: "co-ah, co-ah"

roadrunner: "cooo cooo cooo-ah coo-ah," Mexican
cartoon: *bip-bip* "beep-beep"

eagle: mournful, plaintive

hummingbird: insect-like buzzing of wings

raven

----

forms
pale raven, white raven (feathers reflecting sunlight)

----

traits
beak: "a blade curiously thick and sinister," antique
weapon

----

sound

caw, derisive call, discordant cry, "kaah," harsh
croak, "kloo-klukkruk," "rrock" (playful), squawk

———

wingbeat (sound used to claim territory): pulse,
swish, swoosh, whoosh-hoosh

———

Navajo: "gagee" (talking to humans)

———

Mary Allen, river guide: *"Ah, to be a raven!" Tony*
Angell, ornithologist: *"kwakrackrack" (come fly call) and*
"kukuk" (chase call), *Bernd Heinrich*, ornithologist:
"quorks, quarks, and queeks," Joseph Langland, poet:
"night-black raven," Edgar Allan Poe, writer: *"Nevermore"*

SEASONS

———

dry season, fall equinox, fire season, Indian summer,
monsoon, mud time, off-season, rainy season, river
season, shoulder season, spring equinox, springtime,
summer solstice, winter solstice

PEOPLE

ruins

—

forms
ancestral village, cliff dwelling, cliff hamlet, cliff
house, cliff pueblo, cliff settlement, cliff village,
cliff-guarded refuge, cliffside village, dead city,
granary, great house, great kiva, kiva (ceremonial
chamber, cylindrical chamber), necropolis, plaza,
rooftop hatchway, rooftop terrace, roomblock,
sipapu (spirit hole), ventilator shaft (air vent)

—

chambered walls, clustered rooms, courtyard,
dense pattern, dense-packed rooms, dwelling room,
hull, husk, irregular geometries, jacal (wattle and
daub), keyhole doorway (tau-shaped), moki (Moqui),
rack (destruction, wreckage), rising tiers, roughly-
cored masonry, rubbled remains, ruinfield, shadow
structure (mud outline of previous room), shared
walls, structural units, vestige, viga (overhead
beam, transverse beam, rafter), warren

—

traits
ancestral, cavernous, chindi (haunted), cliff-sheltered,
fragmentary, hand-shaped, hemmed-in, hidden,

hive-like, perforated, rooted, stone-walled, tumbled-down, wild

———

Navajo: *tséyaa kin* "house beneath the rock" and *tsénii' kin* "cliff dwelling"

———

Rose Macaulay, writer: *"stone signatures"* and *"ruin-pleasure,"* **Vincent Scully**, scholar: *"a hive of rectangular volumes,"* **Freya Stark**, writer: *ruins "seemed to belong to the land itself rather than to anything human in it."*

rock art

———

forms
bestiary, cave painting, clan symbol, cowboy glyph, dreamscape, element, figure, form, gallery, geometrics, glyph, graffiti, iconograph, iconography, ideograph, ideogram, image, lunar marker, marking, mural, painted rock, panel, petroglyph, pictogram, picto-graph, picture writing, sign, solar marker, solstice marker, symbol, symbol-map, visual prayer

———

anthropomorph, geoglyph, quadruped, zoomorph

———

traits
abstract, ancient, archaic, aural, calendric, ceremonial, hallucinatory, historic, emblematic, entoptic, ghostly, impressionistic, interactive, linear, metaphoric, mnemonic, mysterious, mythic, naturalistic, otherworldly, polychrome, schematic, scrumbled, shamanic, visionary

———

carved, chipped, cut, engraved, gouged, ground, incised, scratched

———

motion
depict, convey, represent

---

decipher, document, investigate, record, research

Gregory Bateson, anthropologist: *"Art is man's quest for grace,"* **Isadora Duncan**, dancer: *"If I could tell you what it meant, there would be no point in dancing it,"* **Ekkehart Malotki**, linguist: *"The meaning is buried deep in these vanished cultures,"* **Charles Olson**, poet: *"I hunt among stones"*

cowboy

---

forms
badlander, bronc rider, broncbuster, buckaroo, cattle driver, cattleboy, cattleman, cowhand, cowpoke, cowpuncher, drover, hand, hired hand, horsebreaker, horse fighter, horse whisperer, night rider, pardner, puncher, ranch hand, ranchman, rancher, range drifter, range rider, saddle tramp, sagebrusher, side-kick, stockman, top hand, trail boss, trail driver, vaquero, waddy, wrangler

---

greenhorn, tanglefoot, tenderfoot

---

outfit, range crew, roundup crew, trail crew, trail outfit

---

traits
craggy, feral, gaunt, grizzled, raw-boned, rough-hewn, sinewy, unreadable, weather-creased, weather-stunned

---

beaverfelt hat, cow hat, creased hat, felt hat, John
B. Stetson ("John B."), neckerchief, sombrero, spurs
(chingling), war bag

---

buckaroo camp, cow camp, headquarters ranch,
home ranch, line camp (line shack), ranch, spread

---

hacienda, rancho

horse

---

drove, maverick, mustang, remuda, rock horse,
stallion, stampede, stomp, string

---

back in the saddle, can lead a horse to water,
champing at the bit, dead run, don't look a gift horse
in the mouth, don't change horses in the middle of
a stream, free reign, giddy, giddy-up, have to see
a man about a horse, hold your horses, horse sense,
horsing around, in his last tracks, it's a cinch, riding
roughshod

firefighter

---

forms
crew boss, fire boss, fire commander, fire lookout,
rookie ("Ned"), safety officer, slurry pilot, smoke
chaser, smokejumper (jumper), spotter

---

fire crew, helitak crew, hotshot crew, initial-attack
crew, mop-up crew

---

jump spot, fireline (scratch line, swathe), perimeter,
timber landing, water landing

---

motion

attack, battle, beat down, contain, control, deploy,
escape, fight, flank, outrun, quench, smother, snuff,
suppress

Michael Paterniti, writer: *"Big Ernie" (smokejumper fire
god)*, **Walt Smith**, smokejumper: *"going into the black"*

_travel
—

foot
—

forms

abrupt descent, backpack, breakneck descent,
bushwhack, cross-country trek, dayhike, day trip,
dead reckoning, enduro, epic, four-mile gait, huffer,
journey, overnighter, pilgrimage, reconnaissance,
rimmed-up, rimrocked, run-march, shakedown
hike, transit, trek

---

breather, respite, water break

---

traits

off-trail, overland, sidehill, surefooted, tanglefooted

---

motion

angle, backtrack, blitz, boulder hop, boot it, brush-
pop, bushwhack, circle, contour, crest, cross, detour,
edge, explore (look-see, poke around, reconnoiter,
scout), file down, head a canyon, hit the trail, hoof
it, huff, jink (move in sudden turns), journey, ledge-
hop, make tracks, navigate, pace, pound, press,
prowl, push, range, rim-walk, scamper, set out, shag
it, skirt, stride, strike out, thread, top out, traipse,
tramp, travel, traverse, tread, trek, tromp, veer

---

clamber, claw, climb, crab, downclimb, kickstep, rest step, scale, scrabble, scramble

———

amble, linger, lumber, meander, roam, saunter, skate, stroll, waltz, wander

———

collapse, crawl, drag, falter, flog, flounder, grope, hobble, knuckle walk, lag, plod, shamble, shuffle, slog, slump, sprawl, sputter, straggle, stumble, thrash, trudge, wobble

———

bat-up (sleep together for warmth), beddown, bivouac, dry camp, nightcamp, pitch camp, shade-up, shut-eye

———

Navajo: *hozho naninaadoo* "travel in beauty"

———

entrada, *jornada* (a day's waterless journey), *paseo*

———

Australian: "chuff off," New Zealand: "bush bash" (bushwhack)

———

Alfred Henry Lewis, writer: *"skallyhootin'"*

trail

———

forms
backtrail, blind trail, branch trail, cold trail, cross trail, downtrail, foot trail, game trail, side trail, water trail

———

access route, bypass, cattle track, catwalk, cowpath, cutoff, footing, footpath, the going, leg, passage, path, pathway, purchase, route, short cut, stage, switchback, trace, track, traverse, treadway, walkway, zigzag

———

finger-grip route, hand-and-toe route, handhold
climb, handhold route, hands-on scramble, sticky-
foot traverse, toehold route

---

traits
boot-scarred, boot-worn, breakneck, broken, brutal,
circuitous, criss-crossing, cross-canyon, dicey,
dim, diverging, dizzying, faint, grinding, sketchy,
well-trodden, zigzaggy

---

motion
angle back and forth, ascend, climb, contour,
descend, dip, drop, jerk back and forth, meander,
pinchout, switchback, traverse, trend, twist,
whiplash, wiggle, wind, wrap down, zigzag

---

vereda "trail"

Harvey Butchart, hiker: *"ambitious,"* and *"sporty,"*
Dante, poet: *"fool's way"* (path through the land of the
dead), and "hard and perilous track," **Marshall Trimble**,
historian: *"hoot-owl trail"*

backroad

---

forms
all-weather road, comeback curve (wagon teamster
term), double-rut, double-track, dugway, four-wheel
drive road (4WD, 4X), hairpin curve, jeep road,
jeepway, low-gear road, ranch road, roadbed,
roadway, sandtrap, sideroad, spur road, tank trap,
trackway, two-track, washout, wheeltrack road,
winter road

---

traits
arrow-straight, corkscrew, corrugated, cratered,
dead-straight, dirt, faint, graded, gumbo, impassable,

jarring, jolting, lurching, overgrown, primitive,
rock-studded, rough as a cob, rudimentary, rutted,
slickery, tilting, tortuous, twin-rutted, washboard,
washed-out, white-knuckle

———

motion
bog down, curl, high center, jigger, jounce, lurch,
mire, rebound, roll, snake, switchback, twist,
unwind

———

Jean Baudrillard, philosopher: *"desert speed,"* **Hoffman
Birney**, historian: *"tooth-loosening jolts,"* **Dave Edwards**,
photographer: *"Navajo rapids" (Chinle swells, Highway 89)*

river

———

deadman, dry bag (black bag, blag, wet bag), line,
major-powelling (bow-first), portage, put-in, stroke
(back stroke, push stroke, pivot stroke), take-out

———

drift, ender (endo), flip, flush, punch, rocket,
swamp, tailspin

———

boat woman, boatboy, boatgirl, boatman, galley
slave, highsider, kayaker, oarsman, paddler, river
guide, river hag, rafter, raftsman, rower, steersman,
swamper

———

baloney boat, cataract boat, dory, G-rig (Georgie
White), ghost boat, inflatable, J-rig, kayak, raft,
scow, snout rig

———

*Apocalypse Now: "Never get out of the boat unless
you're going all the way,"* **Bill Morse**, kayaker:
*"Walalata!" (shouted by kayakers entering a rapid,
from the Hopi kwalalata "rolling in waves")*

Bibliography

Abbey, Edward. *Slickrock.* Sierra Club, 1971. See also *Desert Solitaire, A Season in the Wilderness.* McGraw Hill, 1968.

Angell, Tony. *Ravens, Crows, Magpies and Jays.* University of Washington, 1978.

Aristophanes. In *Geography of the Imagination,* Guy Davenport. North Point, 1981.

Austin, Mary. *A Mary Austin Reader.* University of Arizona, 1996.

Bachelard, Gaston. *The Poetics of Space,* trans. Maria Jolas. Beacon, 1969.

Bagnold, Ralph. *Libyan Sands, Travels in a Dead World.* Michael Haag, 1987.

Balzac, Honoré de. *A Passion in the Desert.* 1830.

Banham, Reyner. *Scenes in America Deserta.* Gibbs M. Smith, 1982.

Bashō. "The Records of a Weather-exposed Skeleton" and "The Narrow Road to the Deep North," *The Narrow Road to the Deep North and Other Travel Sketches,* trans. Nobuyuki Yuasa. Penguin, 1966.

Bateson, Gregory. *Steps Toward an Ecology of Mind.* Ballantine, 1972.

Baudelaire, Charles. *Charles Baudelaire: Complete Poems,* trans. Walter Martin. Paul & Company, 1998.

Baudrillard, Jean. *Jean Baudrillard: Art and Artefact.* Sage, 1998.

Berger, Bruce. *The Telling Distance.* Breitenbush, 1990. See also *Almost an Island, Travels in Baja California,* University of Arizona, 1998.

Bierce, Ambrose. In *Ambrose Bierce, Alone in Bad Company,* Roy Morris, Jr. Crown, 1995.

Birney, Hoffman. *Roads to Roam.* Penn, 1930.

Black Elk. In *Black Elk Speaks,* John Neihardt. University of Nebraska, 1961.

Bowden, Charles. *Killing the Hidden Waters.* University of Texas, 1977.

Boyle, T. Coraghessan. *Water Music.* Little, Brown, 1981.

Butchart, Harvey. Personal communication, July, 1972.

Carter, Forrest. *The Education of Little Tree.* University of New Mexico, 1986.

Cézanne, Paul. *Cézanne by Himself,* ed. Richard Kendall. Little, Brown, 1988.

Clark, Kenneth. *Landscape into Art.* Beacon, 1961.

Crane, Stephen. "The Bride Comes to Yellow Sky," *The Western Writings of Stephen Crane.* New American Library, 1979.

Crowley, Buck. Personal communication, May, 1988.

Dahlberg, Edward. "The Leafless American," *The Leafless American & other writings.* McPherson, 1986.

Dante (Alighieri). *The Divine Comedy,* trans. John Ciardi. W. W. Norton, 1977.

Davenport, Guy. *Geography of the Imagination.* North Point, 1981.

Dellenbaugh, Frederick. *The Romance of the Colorado River.* Rio Grande, 1904.

Disney, Michael. *The Hidden Universe.* Dent, 1984.

Dixon, Maynard. *Rim-rock and Sage.* California Historical Society, 1977.

Doig, Ivan. *Winter Brothers: A Season at the Edge of America.* Harcourt Brace, 1982.

Duncan, Robert. *A Selected Prose*, ed. Robert Bertholf. New Directions, 1995.

Durrell, Lawrence. *Bitter Lemons.* Dutton, 1957.

Dusard, Jay. Personal communication, April, 1991.

Dutton, Clarence. *Tertiary History of the Grand Cañon District.* Peregrine Smith, 1977.

Dye, Bob. Personal communication, November, 1998 and February, 1999.

Edwards, Dave. Personal communication, April, 1996.

Eiseley, Loren. *The Night Country.* Charles Scribner's Sons, 1971.

Ehrlich, Gretel. *The Solace of Open Spaces.* Penguin, 1986.

Fletcher, Colin. *The Man Who Walked Through Time.* Alfred A. Knopf, 1967.

Flaubert, Gustave. *The Temptation of St. Antony.* Viking, 1983.

Galvin, James. *The Meadow.* Henry Holt, 1992.

Garland, Hamlin. "Among the Moki Indians," *Harpers Weekly* 40, Aug 15, 1896.

Gass, William. *Habitations of the Word: Essays.* Cornell University, 1997.

Goethe, Johann Wolfgang von. *Faust.* W. W. Norton, 1976.

Gregory, Herbert. *The San Juan Country*, Professional Paper 188. U.S. Geological Survey, 1938. See also *The Kaiparowits Region*, Professional Paper 164. U.S. Geological Survey, 1931.

Griffith, James. *Southern Arizona Folk Arts.* University of Arizona, 1988.

Grossinger, Richard. *Spaces Wild & Tame.* Mudra, 1971.

Guthrie, A. B. Jr. *The Big Sky.* William Sloane, 1947.

Hall, Oakley. *Ambrose Bierce and the Queen of Hearts.* University of California, 1998.

Hatcher, Bill. Personal communication, November, 1999.

Haugh, Brad. In "Blow Up," Sebastian Junger, *Men's Journal*, November, 1994.

Havel, Vaclav. *Open Letters*, trans. Paul Wilson. Vintage, 1992.

Heinrich, Bernd. *Ravens in Winter.* Summit, 1989.

Job. *The Book of Job*, ed. Stephen Mitchell. Harperperennial, 1992.

Joubert, Joseph. *The Notebooks of Joseph Joubert*, ed. and trans. Paul Auster. North Point, 1983.

Joyce, James. *Finnegan's Wake.* Viking, 1967.

Kerouac, Jack. *Desolation Angels.* Riverhead, 1995.

Koch, Elers. *Early Days in the Forest Service, Volumes 1–3.* USFS, Missoula, 1944. See also "History of the 1910 Forest Fires in Idaho and Western Montana," manuscript, Lolo National Forest, 1942.

Langer, Susanne. *Mind: An Essay on Human Feeling.* Johns Hopkins, 1974.

Langland, Joseph. *Selections, 1991.* University of Massachusetts, 1991.

Lao-tzu. *Tao Te Ching*, trans. Burton Watson. Hackett, 1993.

Lawrence, D. H. *Mornings in Mexico.* Alfred A. Knopf, 1927. See also *Sea and Sardinia.* Viking, 1962.

Lawrence, T. E. *Seven Pillars of Wisdom.* Doubleday, Doran & Company, 1935.

Lea, Tom. *The Wonderful Country.* Little, Brown, 1952.

Lewis, Alfred Henry. *Wolfville.* Garrett, 1969.

Lomatewama, Ramson. *Silent Winds.* Self published, 1985.

Long, Haniel. *The Power Within Us.* Duell, Sloan and Pearce, 1944.

Lopez, Barry. "Searching for Ancestors," *Outside* April, 1983. See also "Gone Back to Earth," *Crossing Open Ground.* Charles Scribner's Sons, 1988.

Loti, Pierre. *The Desert*, trans. Jay Paul Minn. University of Utah, 1993.

Macaulay, Rose. *Pleasure of Ruins.* Thames & Hudson, 1966.

Maclean, Norman. *A River Runs Through It and Other Stories.* University of Chicago, 1976.

MacLeish, Archibald. In *Way West*, Edward Dorn. Black Sparrow, 1993.

Malotki, Ekkehart. Personal communication, December, 1998.

Madsen, Scott. Personal communication, May, 1987.

McCarthy, Cormac. *Blood Meridian.* Random House, 1985. See also *The Crossing.* Alfred A. Knopf, 1994.

McPhee, John. *Rising from the Plains.* Farrar, Straus and Giroux, 1986. See also *Basin and Range.* Farrar, Straus, Giroux, 1981.

Melford, Michael. Personal communication, August, 1988.

Melville, Herman. *Clarel.* Hendricks House, 1960.

Miller, Henry. *The Colossus of Maroussi.* New Directions, 1941.

Milton, John. *Paradise Lost.* Odyssey, 1935.

Milzer, Scott. Personal communication, March, 1991.

Momaday, N. Scott. *The Way to Rainy Mountain.* University of New Mexico, 1969.

Mudd, Harvey. "True Record," *The Plain of Jars.* Black Sparrow, 1982.

Nabokov, Vladimir. *The Stories of Vladimir Nabokov.* Alfred A. Knopf, 1990.

Newby, Eric. *A Short Walk in the Hindu Kush.* Penguin, 1983.

Nietzsche, Friedrich. *Thus Spoke Zarathustra.* Penguin, 1969.

Olson, Charles. "The Kingfishers," *The Collected Poems of Charles Olson*, ed. George Butterick. University of California, 1987.

Ott, Wallace. Personal communication, May, 1992.

Paterniti, Michael. "Torched," *Outside*, September, 1995.

Poe, Edgar Allan. *Complete Stories and Poems of Edgar Allan Poe.* Doubleday, 1966.

Pound, Ezra. *The Cantos of Ezra Pound.* New Directions, 1996.

Powell, John Wesley. *The Exploration of the Colorado River.* Dover, 1961.

Powell, Walter Clement. "Journal of Walter Clement Powell," ed. Charles Kelly. *Utah Historical Quarterly*, 16, 17 (1–4, 1–4).

Priestly, J. B. *Midnight on the Desert.* Harper and Brothers, 1937.

Rawlins, C. L. *Broken Country: Mountains and Memory.* Henry Holt & Company, 1996.

Reed, John. *Insurgent Mexico.* International, 1969.

Renner, George. Personal communication, June, 1995.

Ruess, Everett. *Wilderness Journals of Everett Ruess*, ed. W. L. Rusho. Gibbs M. Smith, 1998.

Ruskin, John. *Selected Writings*, ed. Kenneth Clark. Penguin, 1992.

Saint Exupéry, Antoine de. *Wind, Sand, and Stars*, trans. Lewis Galantière. Reynal & Hitchcock, 1939.

Schama, Simon. *Rembrandt's Eyes.* Knopf, 1999.

Scully, Vincent. *Pueblo: Mountain, Village, Dance.* Viking, 1975.

Shakespeare, William. "King Lear," *The Complete Works of Shakespeare*, ed. David Bevington. Addison-Wesley, 1997.

Simpson, Elizabeth. *Mountain Lying Down.* Southwest Parks and Monuments, 1989.

Smith, Jedediah. *The Travels of Jedediah Smith*, ed. Maurice Sullivan. University of Nebraska, 1992.

Smith, Walt. Personal communication, June, 1995.

Snyder, Gary. Flagstaff talk, November, 1999.

Stark, Freya. *Letters from Syria.* John Murray, 1943.

Steck, George. *Grand Canyon Loop Hikes I.* Chockstone, 1989.

Stegner, Wallace. *Beyond the Hundredth Meridian.* Houghton Mifflin, 1954.

Steinbeck, John. *The Log from the Sea of Cortez.* Viking, 1951. See also *The Portable Steinbeck*, ed. Pascal Covici. Viking, 1976.

Stevens, Larry. *The Colorado River in Grand Canyon, A Guide.* Red Lake, 1983.

Tagore, Rabindranath. *Gitanjali.* Scribner, 1997.

Thesiger, Wilfred. *Arabian Sands.* Penguin, 1964.

Thompson, Taylor. "Incidents of Ranger Days," *Frontier Times* 1(9), June, 1924.

Trimble, Marshall. *Law of the Gun.* Arizona Highways, 1997.

Turrell, James. *Occluded Front.* Lapis, 1985.

Thoreau, Henry David. *Walden, and other writings*, ed. Brooks Atkinson. Modern Library, 1950.

Van Dyke, John. *The Desert: Further Studies in Natural Appearances.* Scribner's, New York, 1901.

Van Gogh, Vincent. *Dear Theo*, ed. Irving and Jean Stone. Doubleday, 1937.

Vernon, John. *The Great Unknown.* MS.

Waters, Frank. *The Colorado.* Swallow, 1974.

Watts, Peter. *A Dictionary of the Old West, 1850–1900.* Alfred A. Knopf, 1977.

Williams, Terry Tempest. *Coyote's Canyon.* Peregrine Smith, 1994.

Williams, Tony. Personal communication, June, 1994.

Williams, Tyler. Personal communication, April, 1998.

Wister, Owen. *The Virginian: A Horseman of the Plains.* Penguin, 1988.

Wolfe, Thomas. *Look Homeward Angel.* Scribner, 1995.

Wright, Frank Lloyd. In *Frank Lloyd Wright: Architecture and Nature*, Donald Hoffmann. Dover, 1986.

Index